The Confessions of Narcissus

Interludes from Literature and Life

Sean Scully

THE CONFESSIONS OF NARCISSUS:

Interludes from Literature and Life

DALKEY ARCHIVE PRESS

Dallas / Dublin

PB: 978-1-62897-453-9

Ebook: 978-1-62897-480-5
Library of Congress Cataloging-in-Publication Data: Available

Interior design by Anuj Mathur
Cover design by Kit Schulter

www.dalkeyarchive.com
Dallas / Dublin

Printed on permanent/durable acid-free paper.

The Confessions of Narcissus

Interludes from Literature and Life

To Máirín

Having spent a great many years trying to become wise, I have finally come to accept that, if I am very lucky, I might one day be able to bear, with something like equanimity, the tragedies—and the triumphs—of everyday existence.

But I don't expect I will ever be in a position to offer any advice.

I don't quite know what to make of my own life most of the time, so I cannot speak with any authority about the sort of lives that other people should live—or should want to live.

In an age that seems deeply ambivalent about the value of expertise, I find myself falling out of love with "self-help" as a genre.

It has been the fashion of successive ages to regard the artist as an intellectual. Today, we go much further. Mere intellect does not satisfy. Our attention demands a much greater return. It does not matter that a novelist has told a good story; it is of vital importance that a novel should speak to the condition of the country. A novel might forbear to give us giants and witches, but it must not fail to tell us the truth about everything.

Literature, like magic, is both transformative and revelatory. A good sentence is very like a good spell.

Words are precisely what the ritual of writing attempts to uncover. Meaning is therefore a process of unfolding; the value is inextricably wound together with the experience both of writing and of reading. We need not despair over bad introductions.

In the world underground, Alice discovers that what she thinks she knows doesn't quite work and never gets her where she wants to go. Wonderland, in other words, reveals that there is something absurd about our desire—our demand, even—for coherence.

The story is the thing that, whether because it is too painful or too familiar, needs to be broken up, but a story is what the activity of breaking up is always trying to return to.

For better and for worse, stories are what we seem to require and also what we suffer from.

Good art is not a matter of proofs, it is a matter of possibilities. What it offers is a break from certainty. Good art removes us from the life we seem to lead.

This quality has sometimes been called "strangeness"; it means something more than mere difference.

Unlike the flaneur who flits and chooses to be out because his creditors happen to be in, the truly inquisitive spirit is a habitual meanderer, and wanders not because it is right or beautiful to do so, but because his nature compels him, and he can do no other.

Experience is both a foundation and a refuge from the future.

Every successful therapy begins with a surrender; that is why clinicians cannot help being interested in *Hamlet*. Consent to treatment is not a guarantee of success, but for the patient as for the Prince, "the readiness is all."

The riddle of the Sphinx in *Oedipus* is, among other things, about the changing nature of man on his march toward death. The Sphinx has the head of a man because, like a great many men, it is satisfied with mere answers.

Far from being a wise man, Oedipus showed only that he knew a little about how to walk (it was the business of travelling, after all, that got him into trouble in the first place), and nothing at all about how to live.

Uncertainty is not always an ailment. The evacuation of doubt does not have to be the end towards which all mental activity must strive; taking an interest in things for their own sake (and without regard to ourselves) is sometimes the sanest, healthiest thing we can do.

Scientists are not infrequently good artists. They are good artists because they are not afraid to be children. Like children, they look at the world and wonder. Their curiosity is more powerful than their sense of certainty.

It is also more alive.

Art is not a panacea; life is much more than a process of pain management. Everyday life is very often extraordinary; even good art is sometimes very dull.

Self-knowing, if it is a virtue, is not always a cardinal virtue. It can also be a sort of self-parody: a relentless repetition of those aspects of ourselves that are most familiar to us.

Pursued too determinedly, it can become a merciless regimen of self-diagnosis, where the symptoms always feel debilitating and the prognosis is invariably poor.

Modern Warfare, though indistinguishable from Modern Love in most respects, differs from the latter on this one crucial point: only in Modern Warfare are there no restrictions limiting the number of participants who may be engaged at any one time.

He who fights too long against dragons is doing it badly, though still better than some.

What Hamlet's thinking illustrates is that reason is not always a virtue; sometimes, it can be a kind of forlorn idiocy. Hamlet's world only seems small because he is not actually interested in the world.

He is interested only in himself.

Art is a matter of dressing for dinner. Life is the fact of chasing after one's hat.

If art can seem to make life more bearable, it also beguiles us into the belief that real life is not as pleasurable as it might be; it is, perhaps, not as pleasurable as it should be.

Art, in that sense, is soothing, but it is also self-serving. Under the guise of telling us the truth, it can trick us into a condition of dependency. It can cause us to feel worse than the circumstances of our life seem to require.

When William Hazlitt declared, "It is we who are Hamlet," he drew attention to something about Shakespeare's universality that is worth considering: Hamlet does not just give voice to fears and anxieties we hold in common, he also calls them into being.

If words are not always what they seem, and they can (and do) communicate more than we always care to acknowledge, it may be that our aesthetic principles rather than our words are what principally hold us back and make us feel so ill at ease with the stories we are able to tell (and not tell) about ourselves.

It may be that if our principles were more inquisitive than condemnatory, then even bad writing might be of interest.

The man who takes the road less traveled sometimes finds that he has ventured onto private property.

Heathcliff is a changeling, introduced onto the moors under the cover of darkness. Like *Jane Eyre*, *Wuthering Heights* is a story of collision with the world of fairies. But whereas *Jane Eyre* considers what it might be like to live in a world where fairies are possible, *Wuthering Heights* is a dream about what it might be like to try to become a fairy.

Like Chrétien de Troyes's Perceval, we are always on the road to discovering that wisdom is invariably a belated sort of gift, and one that comes to us from a land that is both a place of experience, and also a world of make-believe.

If we sometimes value art over life it is only because we are simple creatures, and art is easier to understand.

One of the freedoms that art affords is that it does not have to be right.

Philosophy, like art, is partly a recognition that everything is interesting, not least because anything might prove to be important.

If 'knowledge' is the term we use for things we think we understand, it is also a way of signaling when and how our thirst has been satisfied.

Knowledge, in other words, tells us something about the sorts of stories we find compelling.

But it also tells us something about the ways we are beguiled by ignorance.

If we are not always what we would wish to be, we are, at least, always more than we seem. Our words have value even when they seem to come out wrong.

Perhaps especially when they seem to come out wrong.

Sometimes, what we think we know is actually what we are suffering from.

Sometimes, what we think we know is what is holding us back and preventing us from having a new experience.

When we claim to know ourselves, it may be that we are really trapping ourselves in whatever self-portrait is easiest to draw. Too much "self-knowledge," in that sense, can be a very dangerous thing.

The true critic does not master art; he is mastered by it.

Art education is not so much a method as a mindset; it is a commitment to the idea that attentiveness is worth trying because the people who make art, and the people who are affected by it, are worthy of our effort.

Real growth is, in part, an art of forgetting; it begins with learning to set to one side.

The desire for growth is in no way a simple idealization. It is an act of conscious risk-taking.

Growth means something more agnostic than mere improvement.

It means accepting that what is worth knowing may take us beyond the limits of our control.

It means willingness to experience the world on someone else's terms.

Reading, like listening, is, among other things, a test of what, and how much, we are able to endure.

And the test of all expertise is resilience.

True knowledge is not rationality above all else, nor is it principally a body of insight about our emotions.

It is that which is able to endure the violence of our passions, the waywardness of our private (and indeed, professional) predilections.

Art is not an aspect of deity. Art appreciation is not akin to godliness.

The lesson of *Oedipus* is that that none of us is as clever as we think we are.

Like Oedipus, what we sometimes suffer from is not blindness but myopia.

Even the philosopher is naked when passion calls.

Reason, far from being an alternative to impulse and credulity, may be something much closer to a genteel co-conspirator.

Under the guise of telling us the truth, it shows us what belief is able to endure (or is willing to accept).

Beneath the fine cloth and bright buttons, it reveals something about the anxieties we are trying to escape.

In Wonderland, word games coexist with the King of Hearts's relief that time needn't be wasted searching for meaning in incomprehensible verses.

The world underground, that is to say, resists dogmatic simplification.

Sometimes, as Alice discovers in the course of her adventures, the judgement is the most nonsensical thing of all.

If art has only testimony to offer, then a work of art may be set aside as soon as its evidence has been taken.

We are never quite masters of our own experience and never less so than when to be heard is what we most urgently require.

A sense of certainty about what we are experiencing can be a dangerous self-deception.

There is, in other words, something undeniably tragic about Oedipus's discovery that he is wedded to his mother; there is, however, something quite comical about it too.

Both aspects are present in the play and serve to remind us that however well-traveled we may be, we are never quite so far from home as we might think.

If our earliest interest in stories were expressions of appetite, our development as readers is a practice of learning not to close the book when we feel we are not getting what we want, when we want it. It is a practice of sticking with words and ideas that do not immediately grip us, and sometimes, never grip us at all.

Opinions do not lose significance because everyone can have one; they are significant precisely because everyone *does* have one.

They are the one form of common currency that allows everyone to participate in the valuation.

Art does not tell us the truth about wardrobes; it reminds us that we should not take wardrobes for granted.

If we cannot (and maybe should not) be absolutely content with ourselves and confident about who we are and what we believe, it may nevertheless be possible to wonder what it would be like to think and read in a way that privileges curiosity above confidence, and even above contentment.

If searching for truth (both about ourselves and about the world around us) causes us to sometimes discover things we would have preferred to remain hidden, it may be that disappointment needn't always be debilitating.

If peace of mind is something we desire, it may be that our desire (our demand, even) for peace of mind is part of what is causing us to feel so fragmented, so at war with ourselves.

The great freedom literature affords is that it does not matter.

Like the knight Perceval, we are always on the road to discovering that what we think we know can only take us so
far, and never quite so far as we would like.

The Picture of Dorian Gray is in no way diminished by the fact that young dandies do not really enter into binding contracts with canvases and paints.

If we cannot quite bring ourselves to believe that the Oedipus play might have been a comedy rather than a tragedy, it is at least possible to believe that it did not have to be as tragic as it was.

What we come to experience as the fundamental sorrow of the drama is not a sorrow of conflicting, conflictual forms of gratification, of a man who found a guilty sort of affection where the innocence of the child had been denied.

The tragedy of Oedipus is principally a tragedy of interpretation: it is a tragedy brought about by his having only one way of looking at the world.

It is the revenge of the riddle upon the man who believes that to master word play is to master mystery itself. It is the exaggerated acting out of a fool's confession.

In Oedipus's account of his own life, Wordsworth's line "The Child is father of the Man" is transformed into a kind of demon shadow that Oedipus will not allow himself to consider escaping. He is overawed by his own interpretation, and so he comes to be dominated by it. He mistakes an idea for the entire truth.

Like so many serious-minded people, Oedipus swims in the shallows of his own discoveries, and mistakes them for an ocean.

He is an explorer who comes to drown in his own bath.

Sometimes, it is not such an easy thing to distinguish a Duchamp from a circumstantial dustbin.

Self-mutilation, in one sense, in the symbolic sense, is a corrective: the breaking up of the self (or some part of the self) is a renunciation of the overbearing model of ourselves that we can only fail to live up to.

As readers, we are left to wonder what the Oedipal story might have been like if Oedipus had not been quite so sure who and what the play was about.

As critics, we are left to wonder whether Oedipus was more like a semi-literate author or merely a dangerously proficient editor of his experience.

As critics, we are left to wonder whether reading is what we should really be doing, or really want to be doing, or whether the act of reading is, in one sense, a way of preempting the possibilities of a conversation, a rigid preference for what has already been written over all that might be said and is still to emerge.

All art is works of art because all art is a matter of detail.

The cycles of history are invariably uniform. Every civilization begins badly and ends bawdy.

Experiments with and questions about authority are one of the ways we learn to make sense of our appetites.

If we not infrequently resent demands that are made of us (the authority of others), it is also true that we sometimes seem to revel in our status as object.

We find fulfillment in a power that looks very much like powerlessness.

When we are not being denied more than we can endure, we seem to be fascinated by the sorts of checks or limits that might be placed on our desires.

In *Jane Eyre* as in the story of Beauty and the Beast, the drama turns on the recognition that what seems to be weakness is really strength in disguise: the seemingly submissive heroine is really the driving, dominating force in the story.

History has no future. It feels the weight of no moral obligation. Like good art, good history is filled with long silences.

Taking an interest in what a child is drawing is far more important than knowing what to say.

It may be that we are more like Creon and Antigone than we are prepared to openly acknowledge: simultaneously king and supplicant, driven and also confused by our desire for authority and for something that is uninhibited, more elemental.

Failure is a fact of life.

"I am a failure" is a defense against further effort.

"Propaganda" is partly a statement about what other people find compelling; it would be something else if it did not seem to be working.

A teacher is one who wishes to share in the joys of discovery.

An "educator" is merely a third-rate sort of dictator.

If accepting advice feels like an admission that we are actually sick, it can also help us to make life more manageable when we are feeling too overwhelmed. It offers an alternative to seemingly limitless confusion.

If authority is something we cannot entirely live without (and possibly should not want to), it is also one of the things that makes life difficult.

When authority is not telling us what we must do, or cannot do, it is not infrequently trying to convince us that authority itself is wholly authoritative, that what it sees and knows is all there is, that the life we lead is all the life there is.

At its worst, it is the story of the child who, like Eve, is punished for breaking the first rule, the only rule she cannot possibly obey, and it is the story of the man who, like Adam, grows up to believe that he is a god, or rather, that he is the God.

Give a man a fish and you feed him for a day.

Teach a man to fish and he will return, cold and despondent, and carrying only an old shoe.

At its best, wisdom is the fact of encountering our own ignorance without being overwhelmed by it.

Learning to read is not unlike learning to listen; like listening, it is the art of attending to words that are difficult and unfamiliar to us (and may even feel threatening).

The lesson of every fairy tale is that we cannot put the world into a box and stand above it; but, if we are imaginative enough, we might be small enough to live comfortably and conveniently in a shoe.

Art reminds us that some of our very best ideas often come to us in the form of a wild dream.

We are, all of us, troubled defenders of the value of reading. When we are not telling ourselves (and other people) what reading adds to our understanding and appreciation of the world around us, we are bemused by the fact that the world around us feels unfamiliar, and far too much for us to bear.

"About" is the epitaph under which the remains of art are buried.

If the critic is a person (or the sort of person) who understands that each of us is an artist, and an artist does not always tell the truth, the critic is also the person who apprehends the danger of his own insight.

Criticism, to the extent that it claims to be authoritative, is always in danger of turning the critic into the person whose claim to have a cure is really a symptom of disease, is always in danger of turning the expert into the most ignorant person in the room.

If we cannot help being quick to acknowledge that words have power, it may be that there is cause to wonder what sort of power words actually have, and what power we want them to have or fear they might have).

We want to speak in our own way and describe life in our own terms, but in the course of living our lives, we frequently find that words seem to abandon us.

And what they abandon us to may be as uncertain as what they abandon us for.

It may be that what we think of as the unconscious is made more or less appealing, seems more or less persuasive, because the alternative interpretations we have seem somehow inadequate.

Instead of a complex, it may be that what we really have is a desire for more capable words.

What we call listening is all too often something much closer to interpretation, which is, itself, a sort of ventriloquism, but a ventriloquism that has forgotten what a doll is, and that a doll is what it is holding.

At its best, the practice of literary criticism is really a practice of learning to listen; first and foremost, it is an art of silences.

As an art, it values availability over authority, which means, among other things, that the critic is the kind of person who takes an interest in other people but isn't entirely sure that he knows what a person is.

Like a player in a Dickensian adventure, the critic extolls humanity precisely because, like Pancks, "that dingy little craft," humanity itself does not seem quite human; it is something much more unexpected, much more mysterious.

The fox knows one thing, and the hedgehog knows one important thing; but the "fretful porpentine" does not know quite so much as it fears, so that that it injures many, but none more so than itself.

When criticism is written down—when it isn't or cannot be a conversation, or a drama—it is something like the fact of strolling down a street or floating down a river, combined with an uncertainty—even an easiness—about where that might take us, and what might happen along the way.

It is the fact of wearing a white tie coupled with the very real prospect of having, shortly, to run after one's hat.

The critic, that is to say, is both entertainer and entertained. Like a player in a farcical comedy, what the critic really knows is that honest conviction is always on the verge of turning into an almighty fall; like the survivor of some great courtly intrigue, he understands that aspiration is always in danger of turning into Macbeth, or worse, Oliver Cromwell, that inside every self-help book is the story of Cain's descent into Hell.

If we think of the overbearing teacher as being the sort of person who interrupts what a child is saying in order to tell the child what she really means, then criticism is both a curiosity about what is being said, and also a wariness about the possibility of being taken in.

It is both a celebration of the individual and also a suspicion that we may be deceiving ourselves when we claim to know who we really are.

It is, in that sense, the very opposite of an idealization.

Whether the beauty of surfaces is diminished by a terrible depth is partly a question of whether or not one can swim and partly a question of the company.

Like Oedipus, what we suffer from is not so much self-estrangement as a certain kind of over-familiarity.

Macbeth is a demon, but his is not a private hell. Unlike Hamlet, Macbeth is fully aware of the existence of other people. More than that, he is interested in them.

His interest is not a matter of altruism; nor is it a matter of idle curiosity. Macbeth is interested in people because he wants what they possess.

We may say that he pays Duncan an equivocal sort of compliment by killing him, but there is no doubt that Macbeth fully understood he was taking a life, in a way that Hamlet, it seems, did not.

A child is necessarily a creative artist, though his choice of canvas is often questionable.

In the modern era, John Calvin might have been a geneticist.

The truth might not set us free, but it does not have to drive us mad. If Camelot, like the court of Oedipus, seemed to fall because the truth was something too terrible to face and too traumatic to survive, then it is worth remembering that the story of Arthur ends with the prospect of a new beginning, that tribulation can be turned into triumph, that if what we experience is sometimes overpowering, it may be that the way in which we experience—the stories we tell ourselves about ourselves—is also important, that we might feel differently if we had a different story to tell, or were not quite so sure we knew what story we were reading.

Art appreciation does not confer special status. A great many people do not enjoy good art.

A great many intelligent people do not enjoy it either.

Readiness is, first and foremost, a surrender of certainty. It means, among other things, receptiveness to all that lies beyond the limits of rationality.

It is also a prerequisite of insight, which goes some way toward illuminating its significance in the story of Hamlet.

Art is long, but science is cheating.

If a stranger happens to tread on our toes, we can assure ourselves that it isn't our fault, that the stranger is a person of dubious character and doubtful parentage, or we can tell ourselves that we are the sort of person who deserves to be stepped on, that we went unnoticed because we are not worth noticing.

When we think of criticism as being a quest for understanding, we sometimes find ourselves believing that life is the sort of thing that really can be decoded and understood, is the sort of thing that can be decoded and understood by us and people like us.

From there, it is but a short step to believing that if a person is not improved by our intervention, the failing is with the other person, and not with our prescription.

Sometimes, it is okay to feel that the story we have been telling ourselves doesn't seem to make very much sense.

Sometimes, what we call the good life is partly an effect of being a very poor artist.

If we cannot help knowing that a churchyard is full of stones, it is also worth remembering that one of these once contained a sword, that within every person is contained the spirit of the man or woman who would be king, that a king may be what we really are, even when we are not at our best.

I set out into the forest, but instead of solitude, I found an old and well-worn path, and as I walked, I found that I was all the better for not being alone.

CPSIA information can be obtained
at www.ICGtesting.com
Printed in the USA
JSHW080712160223
37826JS00005B/5